LIFE IN BUSINESS

EASY WAYS TO WORK LESS, EARN MORE, AND EMBRACE TRUE HAPPINESS

LIBBY LANGLEY

First published in Great Britain 2023 by Purple Star Publishing

Design by Clare McCabe www.purplestardesign.co.uk
Photography by Helen Rowan www.helenrowanphotography.com

ISBN13:   9798374059571

DISCLAIMER

For Jon.
Thank you for living this life in business with me.

Contents

Introduction

There is something deliciously exciting about saying you're an author. That you've written a book. It's a tangible thing that everyone understands.

"You've written a book? Wow. Congratulations!"

It's funny though, because whilst this book is hugely important to me and I am very proud of it (and so grateful to you for being here right now and reading it), the book itself isn't the thing. This book is a culmination of the decade that came before it. A culmination of my life in business so far, and the lessons I have learnt that I can pass on to you.

It's been a long old road to get here, so let me tell you the story of my life in business to this point. Hopefully you will be reassured that whatever you're doing in your business right now is all a perfect part of your own journey...

Prior to starting my business in December 2011 I'd been a career person. In fact, I was a kind of ice queen career person (my team actually used to call me that in my last career job, which at the time was something I wore like a badge of honour). I was focused, I worked hard, I wore the suits, I wore the heels every day and I was a bit of a #bossbabeCEO.

I think that that's what I thought I had to do to get

ahead, and I know there's a lot of perpetuation of that still on social media, but it's not true (a lot more on that throughout this book!).

In my last job before starting my business, I worked in a further education college, and I was responsible for the commercial training side. Whilst I was there, I trained as an adult tutor and I also completed my MBA (my dissertation was about social media marketing strategy, which was kind of edgy back in 2011).

Despite having been hugely successful in my role, having grown the college's commercial income by 218% in three years, I was utterly miserable. I was a commercial person in an educational world, and that disconnect finally came to a point of no return, and I walked out. Simple as that.

Looking back, I would definitely say I had burnout.

It wasn't as widely talked about as it is now, and I didn't recognise the signs, so just ploughed on through until that moment when I snapped.

With no other job to go to, and the gaping hole of a nice management salary to fill, I decided to become the mistress of my own destiny and set up on my own.

I had skills I could utilise. I was a qualified tutor, and had experience in running paid-for workshops, so that was all I needed to get me going.

I knew that I needed to earn money, but that was never the motivator for me. It was about the freedom of time, the experience, being able to spend more time doing things I wanted, working fewer hours, and building a life that suited me and my family.

Knowing what drives you is so important. Yes, you can make an awful lot of money in business, no two ways about it, but that doesn't have to be your sole motivation. What the money brings about is what matters. For most of my clients, the money itself isn't the driver, it's working two to three days a week, fewer hours, and managing their own time. It's working less to earn more. Those are the things that matter to me too.

And so, in December 2011, I launched myself into the world as a bona fide business owner, delivering social media marketing, and business strategy training, and coaching to small business owners.

I earnt money in my first month of trading: albeit only £127! Every step is be celebrated though, and I am forever grateful to the first clients who trusted me to support them.

One thing I did from day one was to get proper support. I didn't have much of a clue about how to run a business, and I wanted to save myself time and energy. Ease has always high on my list of demands for my business, which is why my moniker is now The Queen of Easy Business (a long way from the ice queen!)

One of the places I got support was HMRC. They were running a series of 'how to start a business' workshops locally. I went along and I learned about profit and loss, despite having recently passed finance exams for my MBA. I soon discovered that learning things when you're actually self-employed is very different to learning theory in an educational setting!

I also got coaching through a national programme for entrepreneurs, a year or so into my business. I met lots of like-minded people and discovered what other people were doing in business, and learned things like email systems, and how to set up funnels, and different ways to be really clever in marketing.

Surrounding myself with these like-minded business owners was a game-changer. I met people with so much more experience than me, and absorbed their words and energy like a sponge. *Who you hang around with is one of the things that matters most when you're running your own business,* and this is something I am still conscious of today. I choose the best biz partners, allies, and confidantes I possibly can.

To really up my game, I started going to international conferences, and the first one I went to was Social Media Marketing World, in 2013, in San Diego (I have been to this event six times now). I'd only been in business for just over a year, but right from the start I knew that investing in myself and my business was an important thing to do. That's something I can't tell you enough.

Choose the right conference, choose the right coach, choose the right support, and do invest in yourself, because it makes a huge, huge difference. No investment in yourself will ever be a waste of time or money.

After I'd been in business for 18 months or so, I got my first staff member. One of the things I was told back then was that to be successful, you needed to build a team. I was incredibly busy, coaching business owners, as well doing social media management for companies which was an insane amount of work, so I got an office, employed someone to help me, then I employed someone else, then someone else, and then someone else.

I grew us to a team of five, and the business appeared to be really successful. The turnover was juicy. Profit wise though, things weren't so great. Having an office and having staff is really expensive. I was actually making less profit than I had done when it was me at home on my own. That £127 in my first month had been pretty much all profit, but once I built my "successful business" to a team of five, the profit simply wasn't there.

To me, that's a less successful business. It's a shiny superficial business. And I wasn't happy.

On one of my trips to Social Media Marketing World, I confessed to some of my business buddies that I was miserable and I was basically becoming a manager, like I'd been a manager in the job that I'd left.

Someone said to me "Why don't you stop doing that then?" and it was like a light bulb had gone on for me. Having someone objective on your side can work wonders when you're stuck in a thought-cycle. I came home, made my staff redundant - which was a terrible, terrible time - gave up my office and moved my business back into my spare room.

It was a difficult period, but I had realised a lesson relatively early on in my business: that actually building the business for you is what matters, not the business you 'should' be building.

I started my business because I wanted more time and more freedom to work less, and all I'd done, really, is create the same model as I'd left behind when I'd given up my career.

So, I stepped back and started again.

Mindful of the burnout I'd previously suffered, and to keep everything easy, I actually went into the contracting world for a bit around this time. I took on a couple of big contracts for marketing and business strategy work, which took away some of the freedom and flexibility of being self-employed, but profit wise were great. The ease of the dependability of the work gave me some breathing space during a few difficult personal years (divorce, house move, you know, all those big things!).

But then, the pandemic hit and it allowed me to refocus on what I really wanted.

The quiet of lockdown gave me headspace that just isn't normally there. When you can't go out and you can't do anything, you do just spend a lot more time thinking about what you want to do. And that was a good thing for me (and my wonderful new husband I had married in February 2020).

I decided that I really didn't want to do contract work. I am forever grateful for the opportunities that it gave me, but it had run its course. I knew that it was time for me to step back into my own power.

I wanted to be a coach to business owners. I wanted to make a real difference in the world.

So, during lockdown I created a group business marketing coaching programme, to run fully online. I was no stranger to the online world having run various social media qualifications and training sessions virtually since 2011, but I was aware that the pandemic brought about a shift change in the way business owners thought and worked. It was a more widely accepted way to access things online, and that was a great opportunity I wasn't going to miss out on.

My group programme was successful from day one, but I found it frustrating because in a group setting I couldn't make as much difference as I could one-to-one. Whilst the transformation the group members had in themselves and their businesses was huge, for me, it was a bit unsatisfactory.

It's a strange dichotomy when you've got happy clients but you're not happy yourself. There is always going to be a part of you that says, yeah, but if the clients are happy and it's bringing in money, then stick with it, but the question I asked myself – as I would a client – was *"why am I in business?"*. I, like you I imagine, am in business to make myself happy, to follow my dreams, to make my vision a reality, and to manifest the life that I want. And that means that even if something is successful, if you're not happy with it, you need to change it. And so that's what I did.

I decided to close my group programme in early 2022 and completely focus on one-to-one coaching, because it's the best way I can change people's businesses and lives. I can see in my clients' faces that one sentence I've said is the one sentence that they really needed to hear. It's so rewarding for them and me, and I'm able to invest a lot more energy and support in an individual who's really serious about changing their business, and finding smarter and easier ways to work less and earn more. My clients invest their time and their money in me, and I invest in them – supporting them to grow and develop. It's wonderful; it's mutually very satisfying and I absolutely love it.

With this change of direction, I wanted to change the way I connected with my audience. I have always been active on social media, but I have ongoing frustrations with it (there is a lot more about that in this book!), and I have always regularly emailed my list, and that is something I would absolutely continue, but I wanted more.

And so, here you are, reading my book!

This book, along with my Life In Business podcast, is a new avenue, a new marketing stream, a new way to connect with people, a new way to make a difference.

This feels like a really intimate way to be able to support you and help you. I'm delighted that you're here today and I thank you very much for that.

Let me close by saying that no matter how tough it sometimes gets, there is a reason you're in business. You want to have more freedom, more flexibility, to be the mistress of your own destiny; to be able to control the way that you do things, the hours that you work, and how much you earn. This is the definition of true happiness in business, and that is what matters.

I want you to always remember that the journey is as important as the end goal, and every day brings about some joy of being your own boss. Write down those joys. Celebrate them all.

You are a wonderfully brave human being for daring to step out on your own. Here's to your very successful and happy Life In Business.

Libby x

THIS IS JUST THE BEGINNING

If you're starting out in business, avoiding mistakes and pickles other people have got into is a really smart way to save yourself time and energy from day one.

If you've been in business a while, taking a step back to think about how you actually run your business, and how you feel about it, can never come a day too soon.

The first part of this book will give you the courage to set boundaries; to say no to things that don't help you get where you want to be; and the permission to be as kind and gentle to yourself as you need.

You are seen

The moment you know you have found the one...

The person who you just *have* to work with.

The person who appeals to you because they are a bit scrappy too.

The person who doesn't hide behind filters or fancy graphics.

The person who shows up, despite everything.

The person who keeps it real and shares their vulnerability.

The person who you know you can trust with your business, and your innermost thoughts.

The person who gets inspiring - and realistic - results for their clients.

That heart-stoppingly incredible moment that will change everything.

It's now. You are seen.

Things you don't need

It's important to get this clear right from the start.

You don't need ALL THE THINGS that the Instagram "gurus" tell you need to be successful...

✗ You don't need 10k followers (let's start loving the ones you already have)

✗ You don't need to post daily on socials, unless you want to (what you say matters far more than how often)

✗ You certainly don't need to have your shit together. Take that from someone who's been in business for over a decade and still relies heavily on an army of Post It notes

Take control

What's the point in having a business if you follow someone else's rules?

You're in business because you want more financial independence, time freedom, and joy... right?

So how is sticking to someone else's formula gonna help you achieve that?

In a recent session with a 1:1 client, I asked her why she was focusing on growing an online business when it was making her so unhappy.

She said...

You know what's coming, don't you?

She said: "because that's what we're supposed to do".

There it is. The lack of confidence that stops you shining bright.

Who has the right to dictate what you should do in your business other than you?

No one!

This is your permission to stop following what other people are doing, and create a business that really fills your heart with joy and happiness.

The two things that matter

There are two things in business that aren't talked about enough, but are, in my opinion, the two things that really matter. They are:

1 – HAPPINESS

Do you love what you're doing? Does it make you happy? If not, you can change it...

2 – PROFIT

You'll see loads of online business owners talking about 10k months, and that is generally referring to turnover.

It could have cost them 5k in Ads and staff to achieve that, so their PROFIT is 5k. Profit is ultimately what matters most as it's CASH in the bank.

Know your numbers!

Do you know what your profit margin is?

This isn't about 10k months. This is about a healthy profit margin. The simple way to calculate it is:

Your total income (sales) — all your costs = your profit

Here's an example to make that real for you:

A £10k month with a £9k spend (on ads/staffing/software/etc) is a 10% profit margin (£1k).

A £5k month with £500 of outgoings is a 90% profit margin (£4.5k).

The £5k month gives you more money in your pocket, but that's often not the way it's presented by the "gurus" on Instagram!

Can you see why knowing all your numbers matters so much?

Are you happy?

Do you wake up each morning and think "yes!", or do you have to force yourself out from under your duvet and have ten cups of coffee before you can bring yourself to head to your office, dining table, or wherever you work from?

This isn't about whether or not you are a morning person; this is about your passion.

You see, if you're not passionate about your business then your customers will be able to see this. If you aren't happy, or are bored with your business, your customers will be able to tell. Your customers – and potential customers – are smart cookies and know whether you're being genuine with them or not.

This isn't about you always being shiny, smiley, or polished. Far from it. Sharing your vulnerability and mistakes can be hugely valuable to your followers, and so shouldn't be hidden under a fake veneer.

What I am referring to is a lack of passion for what you do. An underlying feeling of dread. Of misery. Of hatred. Of boredom.

That is NOT good for business, and is certainly isn't good for you!

If you ask yourself whether you love what you do, what is the honest answer?

Is it yes? If so, yay!

Is it no? If so, what can you change to make you love it?

Do you need to outsource some tasks so you can focus on the bits you do enjoy?

Do you need to take a week off and get some headspace if really you're just worn out?

Or is the lack of happiness actually because you're ready for the next step but are a bit stuck on how to get there?

Own your values

Do you have a guiding set of principles and values in your business? It's a great activity to do. Writing this list out will help you remember what you stand for, and keep you away from shiny object syndrome.

My manifesto is simple.

I don't believe in:

✗ Trends and fads
✗ Perfectionism
✗ One size fits all
✗ 24/7 hustle culture

I do believe in:

✓ Goals that matter
✓ Profit over turnover
✓ Working smarter
✓ Putting HAPPINESS first

In business, there is often a lot of the first lot and not enough of the second.

I am on a mission to change that, and I promise that as your guide through this book, I only focus on the things that will make business easier for you.

It's OK to pivot

When I started my business waaaay back in 2011, the advice given to us newbies was to build a team in order to grow to a million pound business. I don't like getting things wrong, so I dutifully did what I was told.

I got an office, I got a team, I had a successful business.

Tick. Tick. Tick.

But it didn't sit right with me. I didn't want to do it like that. I'd had a team in my previous career and I realised I was basically just creating the same structure over again.

Hmmm.

So I changed everything. I gave up my office. I made my staff redundant (the hardest thing I have ever done in my business). I stopped offering social media management (I hated it).

I went back to basics. I focused on working 1:1 with clients and changing their lives.

But then the lure of the corporate contracts came knocking. Great money. Structure. Parental approval (that old chestnut).

But I didn't want to do it like that. I didn't enjoy it. I was bored.

So I ended my lucrative corporate contracts. I started marketing myself again. I re-focused on getting my own clients and changing their lives.

I did what I wanted, and you can too.

It's ok to make it easy.

It's ok to make it fun.

It's ok to do things differently.

It's ok to be scared but do it anyway.

Simple is best

I've been a Wordle fan since the early pre-NY Times buyout days.

I love its simplicity.

One game a day. Five letters. Six guesses.

So simple. So satisfying. So keeps-you-coming-back-for-more.

I think there is a lot we can learn about business from Wordle.

The simpler you make it, the more fun it actually is.

You don't need all the bells and whistles. You just need the core offering, and you need to deliver that well.

And that's it.

Stick to one message. One thing you do. Keep talking about it. Over and over again.

That's how you build a loyal fan base. That's how you grow a successful business.

I've stripped everything out of my business to make it more Wordle-esque.

I have one service: 1:1 coaching, and one message I talk about over and over again: You really can work less and earn more!

And that's it..

What can you simplify to make your business easier, more fun, and more profitable?

5am doesn't define success

5am starts? NO THANK YOU!! That's not for me.

It's also a complete myth that a 5am start is one of the "essential" habits of successful people.

Success is whatever you want it to be, and not having to get up at 5am if you don't want to, could be one definition of success in itself!

It's your business, so run it on your terms.

Nurture the seeds

One spring day, as I was looking out of the window at my blossoming plants, it really struck me how similar growing a garden from scratch is to running a business.

You put the foundations and structure in with your skills, knowledge and experience.

You plant a few things to see what takes.

You move, change, adapt, remove, cut back, and add more of the good things.

You check on it every single day to make sure there aren't any issues, bugs, or damage.

And you take the time to enjoy what you're creating.

Is it ever finished? No.

Does it bring huge amounts of joy? Yes.

Remember: businesses need love, nurturing and patience!

Let's network

DHL delivered a parcel to me the other day.

"I know you", the driver said, as I took the package off him.

I looked at him quizzically.

"You asked a question about the history of this street in the local old pics Facebook group. I recognised your name on the parcel".

I did indeed! And this led to quite an interesting conversation about our shared interest.

When you have your own business, every single conversation is a form of networking. It's how you build your confidence, get to know like-minded people, get new clients, and uncover exciting opportunities.

Yes, even joining a local history FB group is a form of networking. You never know who you will meet, what conversations you will have, and how your life and business will improve through these seemingly inconsequential interactions.

Keep your eyes open to everything.

You never know who you're going to meet next, or who will already know your name...

The problem-solving formula

We can all get stuck when we're trying to solve a problem.

You know what it takes though?

1. **A bit of determination** (knowing you really want to solve the issue, and that it matters to you, means you're more likely to see it though).

2. **A bit of time** (be kind to yourself and don't expect to solve the problem overnight, or even in one go).

3. **A bit of swearing** (this honestly helps in most situations!).

4. **A bit of help** (ask for help in relevant Facebook groups. Reach out to a coach or mentor. Find someone you can outsource to. You never have to do everything by yourself, or suffer in silence).

With that magic formula of four things, you can achieve anything.

Embrace your mistakes

Let me tell you something: you will make loads of mistakes in your business.

You will send out emails with broken links (helloooo! Been there and done that!); you'll muck up your words in a meeting; and your internet will go off in the middle of a Zoom call.

You will make so many mistakes all the time, both in big and small ways.

And you know what? That's all fine.
Mistakes happen. It's how we learn. It's how we grow.

And the sooner you accept that mistakes always happen, the sooner you won't be as bothered to see an unsubscribe, or losing your train of thought, or technology going rogue.

These things won't ever start to feel good, but if you accept them as a normal rite of business passage, then you won't dwell on them, and they won't become a thing that could derail you.

Make it easy

Making things easy is my mission in business and in life (I'm not called The Queen of Easy Business for nothing!).

And recently that translated into me getting not one, but THREE pairs of prescription glasses.

Reading glasses, if you want to be precise about it. Old age. Sigh.

The reason I got three pairs is simple.

It makes my life easier.

I now have one pair for by my bed; one pair with anti-reflective lenses on my desk; and a third pair for in the kitchen.

It's so easy.

I don't need to keep a pair on my head. I don't need to take a pair from the bedroom to my desk, and then curse when I get into bed at night and realise I have left my specs on my desk upstairs.

It just makes life - and therefore running my business - much easier.

It's these little time-savers and ways of being kind to yourself that take the pressure off. It's a way to give yourself just a bit more headspace.

And I'm all for that!

It's time for an audit

How often do you do an audit of what you're spending in your business?

Monthly? Weekly?

NEVER?

It's so straightforward to sign up for software, but then forget to cancel when you no longer use it.

And you could be wasting THOUSANDS each year.

I keep a pretty close eye on my outgoings - my "profit percentage" line in my finance spreadsheet is my favourite thing to look at!

It's because of this, that I recently took the big decision to cancel a course-hosting platform I've been subscribing to for three years, and switch to a more flexible sales page / payment platform.

My business model has changed over the years and so my software and platform requirements have too.

Taking this action will save me £800 in the first year, and about £1200 a year after that, plus it's easier to use for what I need now.

That's a lot of money saved!

I shared this business lesson as a post on social media and got some inspiring comments and messages. One person said:

"I cancelled some unused subscriptions and saved myself £80 a month".

That's nearly a grand a year!

Just for taking a few minutes to audit your expenditure, and without any additional coaching support from me to look deeper and find more!

So, is it time you had a look at your numbers?

It's all in the name

I recently realised something. Two of my clients have changed their names, and I have too. That's three real life examples of business owners actively changing something that doesn't work for them. Something big, too!

Thing is, what you call yourself really does matter.

Inside. Underneath. In your heart.

And if your name doesn't feel right, it might just be the thing that's blocking your success. But you can change it - professionally or personally. Legally or as a trading name.

Client #1 changed her surname because her previous surname was that of her ex-husband, and the new name is really catchy coupled with her first name - and easy to remember - making it great for her business.

Client #2 has started to use her birth surname as her professional name to allow herself a new identity as a business owner without any hangover from her previous career.

I've legally changed my first name to Libby, because it is what I have been called since I was 2. I hated having a different name for formal stuff. It was like there were two of me, which was a pressure I had felt for my whole adult life.

It's really liberating having a name that suits you and where you are in your life and business right now.

So what's in a name? EVERYTHING!

Boundaries matter

It's your business, so you can set your own boundaries!

For me, two client calls in a day is my limit. Each call lasts for 60-90 minutes, and I give my all in that time.

My calls are as exhilarating and rewarding as they are exhausting, and I need to acknowledge that.

These boundaries ensure my energy is balanced. And that I have any energy, full stop!

They also ensure I am able to hold space for my clients, and I can give them everything they need. This includes helping them set their own business boundaries...

Remember – it's your business so you can put any boundaries you like in place.

No need to hustle 24/7, unless you really really want to (I don't, thank you very much).

A boundary lesson

Way back in my early days of business, I used to offer pay-monthly web design services on a commission-only basis for a developer friend. I invoiced the client, paid the developer, and acted as a go-between. Yeah, seeing it in black and white now, it was a terrible idea, but that's not the boundary lesson I want to share here.

I had someone interested in one of these websites, and arranged to go and see her. She then asked to rearrange the meeting to an evening appointment so her husband could be there too. This rang all sorts of alarm bells for me, but I was relatively new to business and so went along with it (boundary #1: fail). All clients are good clients, right? Ha, another BIG lesson there:

All clients are NOT good clients!

I went to the evening meeting, and basically spent the whole time batting away the husband's haggling attempts. He wanted to have two websites for the price of one, which thankfully I stuck to my guns over. Boundary #2: win.

The business arrangement wasn't the smoothest as his expectations were unrealistic. Boundary #3, setting clear expectations: fail. We limped along for a while, and the website was delivered as promised, but it all came to a head one Saturday as I was walking home from a trip into town, through my local park. The husband called me, and ranted about a minor detail on the website that needed fixing. Because I hadn't set clear service expectations, he felt it was ok to call me on a Saturday. (It's also worth noting that he was a truly unpleasant character, and a massive a-hole to boot.)

And so the client-provider relationship ended, not a moment too soon. I ended it actually, in a rush of slightly-too-late boundary setting, and I have never forgotten this horrific experience.

Decide what your terms of service will be and when you are available for calls or emails, and what your response time will be. If clients want you on call 24/7, charge for that! Don't think you have to be at their beck and call all the time: you DO NOT. Especially not on a Saturday.

How to deal with brain-pickers

Do you think you should give time to everyone who wants to "pick your brains"?

Noooooooo! You absolutely DO NOT need to do this FOR FREE.

You are the expert in your field, and it's ok for you to charge for that.

It's great for you to charge for that.

It's right for you to charge for that.

It's safe for you to charge for that.

Instead of feeling guilty and giving up your precious time, offer The Picker a paid-for 1:1 slot, or send them to a link on how to work with you.

You are under no obligation to give away your magic for free.

Isn't that empowering?

Charge what you're worth

A client asked me what they should charge as a day rate. This is a how-long-is-a-piece-of-string type question, but they were embarking on a new venture as a self-employed consultant, and didn't have a clue where to start.

They said they had googled the question and had come up with a figure of £454 a day.

They explained how they had got to that number: annual salary divided by the expected number of days worked (220 is the average) = £454 a day. Hmmmm.

No factoring in for tax. No factoring in for business expenses. And no factoring in for the 20+ years of experience in their field that had led to them being approached to provide this consultancy in the first place.

"Charge £1,500 a day", I said.

They looked at me aghast. "But that's £330,000 a year if I do similar work for 220 days".

Yep. And...?

Why would that be a problem?? Why deliberately

limit the amount you can earn? Why? Why????

Consultants often charge multi-thousands per day because they have the skills, expertise and experience that warrants that investment. And maybe they only work 100 days a year. That's amazing! They have set up their business to support the life they want.

How does that make you feel?

Do you tut and think that no one is worth £1,500 a day, or are you inspired to take a look at your day rate (or the equivalent in your business) and see how much you should be charging for your skills, expertise and experience? I bet you're selling yourself short and there is a little voice inside you that knows this.

Well, now is your time. It is time for you to turn that little voice into a thumping great roar that says I WILL CHARGE WHAT I AM WORTH!

Are you easy to buy from?

"Two forms, both multiple pages. Honestly far too overwhelming. Never going to do it."

Those words are a genuine excerpt from a text I sent my husband about the process to register with a new GP, post-house move. (I did register eventually, but only because I had to. Ugh)

The experience made me wonder how many organisations, services, and businesses lose customers because their sales or sign-on process isn't easy?

I wonder if you're losing customers because of this.

How easy is it for someone to buy from you?

Are your sign-up / buy now links on all your social media channels? In your email signature? Plastered all over your website?

Is the process itself simple? One click? One short form? One easy-to-book-a-call button?

If not.....

EEEEEEEK!!!!

There are a LOT of people like me out there who lose interest or get overwhelmed if it's too hard to buy, and we simply move on to buy or sign up with someone else.

Take a look at your website and social media, and see whether you're easy to buy from, or somewhere on the horrendous GP-registration scale. Be honest now!

You don't need more time

I'm willing to wager that you have said you "haven't got time" to do something, at least once this week.

Amiright?

Thought so.

I get it. Life is busy. It feels like there are always a million things to do. It never ends. And then you throw running a business into the mix and, well, you simply "haven't got time" to even breathe.

Or have you...

I'm willing to wager that it's not time that's the issue here.

It's HEADSPACE.

Not having headspace to think about what needs doing often means things are done in a snatched rush. Half-concentrating. Just getting it off the list before rushing onto the next thing.

But wait...

Everything can be waaaaaaay easier than that!

Here are a few simple strategies you can implement in your business that will give you breathing room and headspace to focus more clearly, and feel less rushed and overwhelmed:

1. <u>Clear communication.</u> If you're allowing your clients to contact you by email, text, WhatsApp, Messenger, Instagram, LinkedIn, and phone, that needs addressing. Pick one line of communication and stick to it religiously. I use Voxer with my clients because it's easy to use (text and voice notes) and it keeps our work separate to conversations with friends and family.

2. <u>Time block.</u> Setting aside days for specific types of work allows you to be in the same mode for longer periods, therefore alleviating the stressful and time-wasting change of focus between tasks, and being far more productive.

3. <u>Set realistic goals.</u> Wanting to earn £100k a year working three days a week is a juicy goal to aim for, and your pricing and max number of clients needs to match that goal. Charging £500 a month for a maximum of six clients at once won't ever get you to where you're wanting to be, so you either need to up your prices or your number of clients, or adjust your income goal to become a work/life balance goal.

It takes a bit of courage to implement these things, but that abundance of headspace and time you can create with a few tweaks is incredibly freeing when you get there.

Listen to good advice

My beautiful Whistles cardigan needed a bit of a freshen up.

Hand wash only, said the instructions.

Nah, said me. It'll be fine in the machine on a low temp. I can make the rules. I am my own woman.

Ahem.

It's still just about wearable (is it though?!), but it's certainly not the result I hoped for. Sob.

Same goes for trying to run a business without support. You can try All The Things, and have reasonable success, but having someone by your side who has been there and ruined the cardie, is invaluable.

You will achieve your goals much more quickly.

And you won't kick yourself for not listening to advice sooner.

Said with love by me, who has been there and ruined the cardigan both metaphorically in business, and literally in life.

If you don't know, ask!

Whilst on a summer holiday in France, my husband and I were woken up by a strange beeping noise.

11pm, 1am, 4am. Beep. Beep. Beep.

Regular as clockwork, continuing for five or more minutes at a time. Then, silence.

So odd. Why would a lorry need to reverse for such a long time? Why would it need to drive round every night? Why in the night at all?

One morning, curiosity got the better of me, and I mustered my best French to go and ask someone what the beeping was.

And so in have-a-go French, I questioned: dans la nuit, quelle est la *beep beep beep*?

Thankfully the staff understood my question (phew).

"C'est un oiseau" they informed me.

A bird?? What kind of bird emulates a reversing lorry at 4am? Well, thanks to Google I now know it's a Eurasian scops owl. And it beeps.

Why it's affectionately known locally as a "petit juke" I don't know. A juke box it ain't. A beeping (geddit?!) nuisance it is, more like.

I wanted to tell you about this because it's an important lesson in life and in business:

If you don't know...

...ASK!

Even if you don't speak the language or know the terminology, or even really know what question it is you're asking, people are always willing to help you.

Don't stay in the darkness, cursing (imaginary) lorry drivers for their selfish behaviour. Find out the answers.

Ask, learn, grow.

Change your perspective

Sometimes when you're struggling or feeling stuck, a different outlook is all you need to get you back on track.

This could literally be moving your desk to a new position like I did recently (I now look out of the window at the trees and sky instead of at a wall...)

Or it could be going for a walk, listening to a podcast, or having a conversation with someone who's got your back.

Whatever you choose to do, the sooner you consider a different perspective, the sooner you will move forward towards your goal.

Remember your vision

Ain't gonna lie, my clients' heads - probably like yours - are busy old places.

What shall I do next?

She's doing that, so should I?

How do I...?

Can I skip this bit?

I need to do more of X

Is my branding right?

Shall I create something else?

Aaaargh!!!

It's easy to get yourself stuck by the constant drive to do more, be bigger, be better, and that causes you to lose sight of what really matters to you...

...the reason you started your business in the first place.

That's what matters!

Your vision. Your path.

The truth about business

Running a business is HARD.

It's lonely.
It's exhausting.
It's mentally and physically draining.
There's no respite.
Your mind never switches off...

But would you change it for the world?

Nah, me neither

MINDSET MATTERS

When you work alone, it's all too easy to get lost inside your own head and start to second guess every tiny little thing you think or do. Or even worse – to believe everything you see on Instagram that you "must" do in order to be successful.

This section will help you to be more confident in yourself and be brave enough to follow your own path towards your big dream.

Stay in your comfort zone

There's a lot of talk in the coaching world about getting out of your comfort zone in order to reach your goals.

Hmm. I think that's nonsense.

As that well-shared meme says, it's called a comfort zone for a reason.

This isn't about never making changes or moving forward.

This is about making changes that you are comfortable with.

They could be lots of small steps, or one giant leap.

As long as you are comfortable with whatever change you make, you will stick with it, and be ready for the next change far sooner than if you're waaaaaaay out of alignment with yourself.

It's the easiest, most gentle, and most successful way to reach your goals.

When you allow yourself to truly be comfortable with change, that's when the magic happens.

Get comfy, and let's begin...

Your recipe for success

In case you'd forgotten.... you don't need:

✗ complicated tech
✗ a big social media following
✗ a team of people
✗ to know all the answers

You DO need -

✓ a really clear vision
✓ to want it to work
✓ to put in the effort
✓ to enjoy what you're doing!

You don't have to hustle 24/7

I don't want to hustle 24/7. I started my business back in 2011 to get away from that, so hustle I won't!

I don't want my clients to hustle either. Everything I help people with is about easy progress, simplicity, and sustainable growth.

Most of my clients have the goal to replace their old full-time salary by working 2-3 days a week – not grow a million-pound empire - and my job as their coach is to help them get there.

It's not about 10k months no matter what, it's about maximising your profit to have the most rewarding business you possibly can, that you run entirely on your terms.

Work less and earn more!

F*** it

I have decided it's time to accept myself for the beautiful mess that I am.

I have the most wonderful husband in the world, a pretty groovy kitty cat, AND I get amazing results for my clients (hello to my fabulous 1:1 client who's now working two days a week for the same income as she used to get in five!)

And one of the reasons I can achieve all that is because of what I have experienced along the way.

Because of who I am. Beautiful mess that that is.

What about you? Are you embracing yourself, or still beating yourself up over something you think you 'should' be instead?

Being unkind to yourself sucks. It hurts. It's counterproductive.

And yet we all do it.

Now is the time to take a breath, and just say...

"Fuck it. This is who I am, and I am a pretty awesome human".

Note to self

Say this in the mirror to yourself every day:

You're gorgeous
You're literally gorgeous

True happiness starts with loving yourself.

Let's break the norm

I like to work from my phone. I like to work in bed.

Being able to act on ideas as soon as I have them makes me a far better coach and mentor to my clients.

Helping a client unpick an issue that's blocking them, using voice notes while I'm cosy and comfortable in my pyjamas works for both of us...

Remember – you don't need the norms; you need what makes you happy.

And if that's doing your best work from your bed, I say hell yeah!

The benefits of taking time out

Taking time out is possibly the most productive thing you can do for your business.

Think about it: if you're "doing" all the time, how can new ideas formulate?

You need headspace to move forward.

You need peace and calm to get clarity.

You need rest to take the next steps.

Give yourself the best chance in business and make space for time out.

The more you allow yourself to relax, the easier it all becomes.

A quick way to get some headspace

I often get asked how to stop all the noise. You know, the NOISE that massively invades your headspace...

Truth is, we have all suffered with having too many things in our heads and not achieving anything because we simply don't know what to do next.

Here's some simple advice for you:

- Write down what really matters to you. The clearer you are on this, the easier it is to stop seeing all those distractions and shiny objects you just need to have a liiiiiittle look at for a minute...

- Focus on what really matters and nothing else. If you're laser-focused on your goal, it doesn't mean you have to hustle 24/7 (ugh, no thanks!), it just means you have proper clarity about what you're doing.

- Say no to everything that doesn't match what really matters to you. It might sound brutal, but will spending half a day learning a new Insta Reels trend really make any difference to you achieving your goal?

Why not put a little sticky note on this page so you can easily find it the next time you feel you need a little headspace?

Prioritise your health

Once, when I had just arrived home from Social Media Marketing World in San Diego, instead of having a long-awaited shower and going to bed, I ended up in hospital.

It wasn't quite the end to my trip to the States that I hoped for, but two ambulances, two shots of adrenaline, several ECGs, a nebuliser, forced oxygen, a few blood tests in hospital, and 12 hours' sleep, and I was fine, thankfully.

It scared me though, and reminded me how important it is to take care of ourselves. Always.

Never put anything before your own health.

Without that you have nothing.

It's ok to take a break

When I moved house in 2022, I more or less took two weeks off social media. I didn't intend to, but moving house is all-consuming and exhausting, and so I didn't do much other than welcome two wonderful new clients, and keep things ticking over.

I'm normally someone who is really present on social media, so it was a bit weird not being there.

But, I needed the time and energy for other things (a billion trips to the tip and B&Q for one!), and to allow space for me and my new clients to get to know each other.

And you know what, time away from social media is fine. It is NOT your life.

It's ok to focus on other things. **It's ok to prioritise.** It's ok to have a little breather.

Do what makes you happy

Whilst on a holiday, I was alone at the pool apart from a woman somewhere in her 70s, who was chilling out and reading her book.

Instead of sedately joining her in reading, I went on the water slide.

Five times in a row!

Why?

Because I wanted to. Because it made me incredibly happy.

Did I care that I was 47? NO!
Did I care that it was a bit silly? Hell NO!

It made me so happy and that's all that matters.

Even the older woman looked up from her book after my third splash landing and grinned.

See, happiness is infectious.

The more you do what makes you happy, the more other people are drawn to you.

It's the same in your business. If you're genuinely loving it, you will attract the right people and your business will flourish.

Be silly for a moment

There is not much that beats the simple pleasure of spinning round on a chair, but how often do we actually take ten seconds out of our day to do that?

Wouldn't life be happier if we span more often?

I say it's time to have a little more fun. Are you with me?

What separates you from the competition?

Competition? No thanks!

Connection, collaboration, and conversation? YES PLEASE!

I don't have any competition because I am the only me.

You don't have any competition because you're the only YOU.

Do business your way, and don't worry about what anyone else is doing.

I promise you this change in thought-pattern will make it all a lot more fun and a lot more successful.

Who are you, really?

You know, for YEARS, I was trying to be someone else.

I felt I had to be this hard-ass career bitch to get ahead. That seemed to be the only way to do it. Be more masculine. Being feminine is a sign of weakness.

My team in my last career job even called me The Ice Queen. I wore this moniker like a badge honour. No one could get to me. I was tough. I got shit done. I moved up the ladder.

WTAF?

It doesn't sound good, looking back.

Thing is, I didn't stop. I carried this on for the first few years of my entrepreneurial journey. To be a success you have to be hard as nails. No room for error. No vulnerability.

And yeah, it worked. My business was a huge success. I helped thousands of business owners do things better.

Was I happy though?

NO. Pure and simple. I was doing what I thought I had to do to be a success, but I wasn't fulfilled.

And quite frankly, all that bad-ass bitch lark is EXHAUSTING. I'm actually really sensitive and caring, but I didn't let anyone see that side of me. I know this was reflected in my work too. I could teach you all the facts and how-tos, but let's leave emotion at the door, thank you.

This led not only to me to be unfulfilled, but also my clients and students not being nurtured to grow and transform as much as I know they could.

And so I gave myself permission to be me, and to shine as the person I really am.

Are you really being you, or the you that you think you should be?

When you've tried everything

The feeling when you have "tried everything" but still aren't where you want to be is horrible.

You feel frustrated.
You feel angry.
You feel like giving up.

But hang on...

Have you actually tried EVERYTHING?

How about stepping back and looking at your business from another angle?

How about trying a bit less hard and seeing where being chill takes you?

How about asking for support and guidance?

How about working with a coach to get you through this sticky patch?

There are so many less stressful ways to grow your business than "trying everything" and hoping something sticks.

You do you

When I started out, I made the decision I wanted to trade under a brand name and not my own. I think I thought a brand name would make me sound bigger and better than I actually was (looking back this was really a confidence issue...)

Over the years I realised people always knew me by my name anyway, so the brand name wasn't needed. In 2018, I finally came out from the shadows, ditched the brand, and used my own name for my business.

I was scared at first, but knew I was leading by the right example to my clients, and the right thing for me. I was the business, so why not just call it by my name?

It is ok to be yourself from day one.

You DO NOT need to pretend you're anything other than yourself, even if you work at home, on your own, with only your cat for company.

The more you are open and honest about who you are, the more you will attract like-minded people. And that really is an incredibly powerful thing.

Trust your gut instinct

Call it intuition, call it a sign from the universe, call it an inkling, call it whatever you choose, but...

DO NOT IGNORE IT!!

Listening to yourself and your inner voice is possibly the single best thing you will EVER do in your business.

Why?

Because you know what is right for YOU, and no one else does. There are lots of people who can teach you tools and techniques in order to achieve something, and lots more people who can help you tap into working out what you really want to do with your business, but ultimately it is only YOU who can decide if that is what you want for your business.

And that is something so precious. Your business is just that: YOUR business. You must run it in a way that suits you. You must defy all convention if you've tried the "norm" and it doesn't work for you. How you feel running your business is everything.

So whatever decisions you make today, before you make them, take a deep breath, trust your gut instinct, and ask yourself...

"How does this make me feel?"

Your happiness matters

If you're happy in what you're doing, putting in the graft often doesn't *feel* like hard work.

And that's the magic of knowing you're in the right place, doing the right thing for you, right now.

What would you tell younger you?

I would definitely tell the younger me to live the life and make the choices that suit me, not what I thought was expected of me.

I could have made life (especially my 20s) so much more enjoyable if I hadn't made choices based on expectation.

Thankfully now I make the choices I want, and to hell with what anyone else thinks.

What would you tell younger you?

Fear is ok

Straight up: I am terrified of horror films. I am actually even scared of the dark... So what was a person like me doing in the cinema, back in 1999, sitting down to watch The Blair Witch Project?

Well, I say "watch", but I spent the majority of that 121 minutes with my hands over my ears (fact: they can't get you if your ears are covered) and my eyes closed.

I was genuinely petrified.

And don't even get me started on when I went to watch Candyman, over 30 years ago now (whaaaat??). I nearly threw up with fear when we had to go back to the multi-storey car park afterwards, and I STILL sometimes have to stop myself thinking 'the words' (three times) when I look in the mirror.

So yeah, me and horror films aren't a match made in heaven.

But you know what I also know to be true? They are just films. They aren't real. My FEAR is real, but that's a construct in my own head, and therefore something I can also deconstruct.

Running a business is also one big scare after another, isn't it?

Every time something doesn't go according to plan, you might think that there's a killer on the loose, ready to slice your business into pieces. But in reality, that killer is only what we BELIEVE is real.

- Zoom cutting out while you're mid-presentation
- Clients cancelling contracts before you've even started work
- Nasty replies to your well-crafted emails
- Spilling tea on your laptop

These are all real things that happen every day in business...

...but they are just rites of passage that don't mean anything about you.

You can choose to recognise that the emotions you're feeling are your own inner fear, acknowledge the feelings, and then do it anyway.

The more you take these horror bumps in your stride, the closer you will be to having the business and living the life of your dreams, not nightmares...

Shit happens

Running a business is the hardest thing you can ever choose to do. Fact.

It's perfectly normal to start the day super positive, and be sobbing near-uncontrollable tears by 11:30am...

We need to normalise that, and I want you to know that I see you and understand you.

Thing is, if you know you're on the right path with your business, and you have the support of a coach (oh, hi...), then those tears and wobbles are a natural part of the journey.

If you're trying to do it alone, those tears can completely derail you and set you back, or off in the wrong direction completely.

It's hard enough as it is, don't make it harder by not getting support.

Someone you can talk to, to sanity check your thoughts is worth their weight in gold, trust me.

Tear up the rulebook

Has your life been built on structure, routine, and rules? Are you so used to the corporate way of doing things, that it's hard to do anything different now you have your own business?

Many of the conscious or unconscious rules you may have are actually brought about by fear.

Things like:

- You need to make an Instagram reel every day or you'll never get new clients (a big lie brought to you by the people on Insta spouting this rubbish).

- You can only email your list at 1pm on a Saturday (which can lead to formulaic content and missing out on sharing juicy stories).

- You have to sit at your desk until at least 3pm or you'll never reach your goals (umm, what?).

Who made these ridiculous rules???

Oh yeah, it was you...

But no more. You are a creative free-thinker, and those rules were only hampering the incredible work you do.

Freedom and flexibility are why you started your business in the first place!

Doing things that make you happy, is the ONLY way to do things. Who cares if that's unconventional?

If it works for you, and it works for your clients...

...that is ALL that matters.

Stop yourself from drowning

As I was sitting by the pool on another hot day on holiday, I noticed a couple of teenage lads looking intently at the edge of the pool.

Lifting the corner of my massive floppy sun hat, I took a closer look at what was going on.

Turns out there was a bee stranded on the overflow edge, between the water and the poolside.

My French is good enough to understand that the lads were concerned.

They were cheering this little bee on, with gentle coaxes of "allez, allez!"

The little fella was gradually walking his way down the pool edge, but it was clear he was really struggling.

"Nooooooo! Il est mort" one of the lads said with sorrow.

But no, the trooper bee was not dead, he was clearly just absolutely worn out.

The older of the two boys got out of the pool and broke off a bit of conifer to try and use as a floatation aid.

A few minutes later, they exclaimed "succés!", and then a massive whoop of "le voilà!" as the bee mustered all his energy and flew away.

The lads high-fived each other in the pool, and honestly their joy at saving that bee was one of the most wholesome and heart-warming things I have ever seen.

And it made me think.

Getting business support is so much like being that bee:

- You want to stop yourself from drowning but can't get out of the hole, despite the people cheering you on from the sidelines.

- You think you're going under, and then you're given the One Thing you need to do it differently.

- **You can breathe at last.** And off you fly.

Being coached can be a challenging and uncomfortable process, but the high-fives of joy as you see success are worth every ounce of hard work.

Feelin' triggered?

If someone on social media triggers you, and makes you feel upset, angry, uncomfortable, frustrated, or sad...

...here are three actions you can take to stay in control

1. MUTE THEM
If the content being shared by this person right now is triggering you, you can mute them. Instagram allows you to mute just Stories, or posts and Stories. You can unmute at any time.

2. UNFOLLOW THEM
Realised this person isn't enhancing your life and you'd actually be happier and more positive without them? Unfollowing only takes one click and you won't see any more of their content, but they might still see yours if they follow you.

3. BLOCK THEM
If you don't want anything more to do with this person, and don't want them to have anything to do with you, you can block them totally. It'll be like they disappeared from the interweb totally.

Don't waste your energy on this.

You're always in control, so you can get on with focusing on what matters most to you.

Be more ladylike

Have you ever been told you should "behave like a lady" or "stick to your own lane"...

It makes me want to throw up.

Women aren't second class citizens.

We are incredible human beings, doing incredible things with our businesses.

Can we just skip to the easy stuff?

With every single client I work with - no exception - the stuff we talk about in our first few sessions is HARD.

Soul-searching questions. Total honesty about how you feel and what you want. Admitting what you really don't like. Looking at what's worked and what hasn't, and why.

There are often tears, but as we peel back the layers so the shape of your perfect business emerges, those tears turn to sighs of relief.

It's really magical to watch, and as my client Kate said: "it's transformative". I love being a part of this process.

You have to do the hard stuff first or the easy stuff that comes afterwards won't be easy at all.

That's the process, and that's how you make the magic happen.

Vulnerability, honesty, and a total lack of mojo

Have I told you about the time I lost my business mojo?

I mean, like, TOTALLY lost it to such an extent that I spent three solid weeks doing nothing but binge-watching box sets (all seasons of Scandal, and Banshee, if you're wondering).

I had been in business for three years or so, and had been very successful. I'd worked with thousands of business owners. I'd achieved the hallowed six-figure (turnover) year. On paper I had everything I'd worked towards.

So where was my mojo?

Well, something happened that derailed me totally. Nothing to do with my business, but EVERYTHING to do with ME.

I got divorced, and it utterly derailed me.

So I just stopped. Stopped doing anything.

For three whole weeks.

I was lost in life, and that meant I was lost in business. You can't detach the two when you're self-employed.

I had no idea what to do. I couldn't think straight. But then my acupuncturist (and trusted friend) said something that changed everything.

"Why don't you buy your ex out and keep the house?"

LIGHTBULB! I hadn't even considered that because I was on my own and self-employed and the banks don't always like that combo.

But now I had a plan. I had something I could get my teeth into. I had motivation. Mojo.

My life was back on track. My BUSINESS was definitely back on track and the next year netted me an 83% profit margin (my best ever!).

But if I hadn't have sought out and listened to the counsel I was offered, who knows where I would be today?

I can honestly say with my hand on my heart, seeking support is the best thing I have ever done for my health, my sanity, and my business.

Remember – never give up, because there is always someone who has got your back.

Collaboration not competition

How many business coaches are there out there? Several million, at a rough guess.

Does that make us all competitors?

Hell no! It gives us the power of more more more!

I've guested on other coaches' podcasts, and I've had coaches join my programmes. Many of my 1:1 clients are coaches.

Why?

Because being supportive is better than bringing other women down.

If you see someone else doing something similar to you, DM them and say hello! You never know what wonderful collaboration or friendship might come out of it.

Footballer by day, engineer by night

In case you missed it, in 2022 England won the Euros.

England's WOMEN won the Euros, I should say.

And that is so much more important than just the trophy.

It's an inspiration for a generation. It's concrete proof that women can, in fact, do "men's things". And WIN!!

(Something the men couldn't achieve at Euro 2020…)

We were away at a festival when the match was on, but managed to watch the magic happen on our phones.

A woman and her nine-year-old daughter caught sight of us watching and plonked themselves down on our picnic blanket.

The daughter almost brought me to tears with what she said.

She plays football at primary school, but the training has been stopped for the girls' team because the focus was on the boys'.

This made her mad.

She said she hopes the fact the women have won the Euros (and the men didn't) will change this.

She wants to be a footballer.

She also wants to be an engineer.

This girl is the exact reason why this tournament matters so much.

She was going to go back to school after the summer and demand the girls' training is reinstated. "How else will I get to play professionally?" she asked me in earnest.

Women are still not on an even keel with men in far too many ways, but things like the Euros tournament will go some way to change that.

Don't ever think you can't do something because of your identified gender.

You too can be a footballer by day and an engineer by night.

The world is whatever you want it to be.

Go and get it!

Change your mind if you want

Over my first ten years in business, I offered (almost!) countless services, and changed my mind on most of them. These included:

1. Social media management services for Facebook, Twitter, and Pinterest (the initial lifeblood of my business)

2. Pay-monthly web design (a six-month dissatisfaction, that you now know the story of)

3. A BTEC in Social Media for Business qualification (run twice, to great success)

4. A social media awards evening (run annually three times, with a glitzy venue and celebrity speakers. A real jewel in my business crown, but very hard work to organise and manage)

5. A social media membership club (all online in the early days of digital business, complete with a bespoke online portal)

6. A monthly marketing magazine (created for approximately 18 months. Printed on beautiful glossy paper and posted out)

7. A weekly column in the local newspaper; a monthly column in a magazine for driving instructors (15,000 copies p/m); and a monthly guest blog post on an online business magazine

site. (I have always loved writing, but these things just ran their natural course)

8. Countless training courses and coaching for companies and business groups (covering a whole host of biz topics, helping about 6,000 people).

And probably a few more things I have subsequently forgotten about...

When you look at that list, that's a hell of a lot of experience, expertise, and knowledge gained over the last decade.

Would I have got all that experience if I hadn't have changed my mind? I doubt it.

Would I now be such a supportive and confident coach to my clients? Definitely not.

Part of being an entrepreneur is about finding what works best for you

...and the only way to do that is to try things out, and change your mind if they're not right or they have run their course.

That's what makes it all so much fun!

The dying art of being nice

Do you think you can get ahead in life or business simply by being nice? Or do you need to be a ball-breaker to truly succeed?

It's an interesting question, and the latter is what social media seems to suggest is the only way. You know, the 24/7 hustle culture, work work work, drive and thrive, ad infinitum...

I don't agree.

Being nice is what really matters in life. Being nice, being kind, being interested is what will get you ahead.

Sure, success takes hard work and determination, but...

you don't have to be a bitch to achieve your goals.

The more goodness and kindness - and care - you project, the more you will attract loyalty and opportunity. The more people will want to talk to you. They more they will want to work with you. The better a reputation you will have.

It's the economics of niceness.

Being nice isn't a weakness. It isn't about giving everything away for nothing. It's about not being so single-mindedly focused on achieving that you forget there is a lot of joy and happiness to be found along the way.

This week, take a minute or two just to chat with someone. Ask them a question about their life, their pets, their weekend.

It's those niceties that will lead to long-lasting and rewarding connections, not the times when you're pushing for a sale.

Scared? Ask anyway

On a holiday in the south east of France, it was every bit as glorious as you might imagine: sunshine, clear blue lakes, mountains, toads...

Wait, what?

Yeah, turns out there were some big old toady buggers there.

I didn't think I minded the croaky things too much, until I encountered one where I least expected...

...outside my shower cubicle. One of the very real perils of camping au plein aire, it seems.

Needless to say, I chose another cubicle, showered quickly, and left asap.

Later that day, I peeked a look, and the huge toady beast was still there. He looked a bit dry and fed up, and I knew I couldn't leave him to wither and die.

So I asked for help.

In broken French (my A-level skipped this particular conversation), I went into the office and explained there was a problem that I needed help with. Not knowing the word for toad, I ribbited. She thankfully understood, assured me it was a common problem (yikes!), and that they would rehome the poor chap.

Phew.

It got me thinking about business though. How often do you encounter a big scary problem, but ignore it, hoping it will just go away of its own accord? It doesn't though, does it?

Sometimes you really need to ask for help.

And then turns out loads of people have the same issue as you, and it's easy to solve, and what were you worrying about it so much for? Why didn't you ask for support sooner?

Are you addicted?

Sometimes we get addicted to the feeling of being stressed. It's not deliberate, but it's what we know, and so letting go of that stress means letting go of part of "us".

Except it doesn't...

Stress doesn't define you.

You don't thrive on it.

It's unhealthy and counterproductive.

It leads you to make decisions in a panic. It leads you to not actually do anything. It leads you to question yourself when things aren't going the way you hoped.

Stress is a BAD thing.

"Just think of the money"

Whenever I was having a shitty day at work, particularly back in my 20s and early 30s when I was building my career, my mum would always say to me:

"Just think of the money".

When you're heading up the career ladder, that advice can work to a certain extent, as whatever it was that had made me feel unhappy would generally pass (until the next time!), and I would get paid, take my annual leave, and add to my pension pot.

But if ever I had a bad day running my business, with a client or contract, Mum would still say the same thing.

"Just think of the money".

And that really riled me.

Why would you do anything in your own business just for the money?

Why work with horrible clients?

Why take on contracts you really don't want to do?

Why forget all your boundaries?

Just for the money?? (you might as well get a job and get the guaranteed salary, annual leave, and pension)

It was with my mum's words ringing in my ears that - several years ago - I vowed to only do the work I wanted to do in MY business.

No more delivering face-to-face training on a Saturday. Ugh. Yep, been there and done that, more than once.

No more going to client meetings at 8am. Ugh. Yep, agreed to too many of those.

No more missing days of my holiday to deal with "urgent" client things that actually didn't really matter. Ugh. Almost ruined a precious weekend away with friends because of my lack of clear boundaries here.

I've been there and done all that, so here's my experience-based advice to you:

Think of yourself. Think of the fun. Think of the experience. Think of the journey. Think of the people. Think of the magic. Think of the opportunity. Think of the joy.

And only then think of the money.

Remember it's YOUR business

One of the most challenging things about being in the online space is the amount of noise and distraction. There are so many promises of "better" ways to do things, and "shortcuts" to million-pound businesses. And most of them are complete crap.

The main issue I have with promises like this is that they don't take into account the fact everyone is starting from a different ground zero.

If two people in the same industry both sign up for a programme that promises a shortcut to a million, and one's entry point is ten years' experience and a consistent £500k turnover; and the other's is a year's experience and a £20k turnover, their end result can't possibly be the same.

That doesn't invalidate the programme's content, it invalidates the programme's PROMISE.

And that's where things start to come unstuck for solopreneurs. You see the shiny lights around the big promises, and think this is your saviour.

You know what though? You don't need shiny lights, or any kind of saviour. What you need is a step back, a deep breath, and a channelling of that inner confidence you have. Somewhere. Deep inside you.

You also need to remember that your business is just that: YOUR business. Every bit as individual as you are.

One size will never fit all.

What you like and dislike matters more than you perhaps give credence to. You started your business for a reason, and trying to fit into someone else's mould of what a business "should" look like is only going to cause you stress, demotivation, and misery.

Be proud of yourself. Be proud of your business. And never feel you need to change any of it, unless you really want to.

When life gives you lemons

There is always shit that will hit you when you run a business.

When that happens, you can...

Give up, or

Accept it as a rite of passage, and MOVE ON towards achieving your goals.

Which one will you choose?

Don't lose sight of you

It's easy to feel like you're missing something when it comes to running your business.

- You're too busy to experience the freedom you crave

- You're not making the progress you wanted despite putting in tons of effort

- You have highs, but too many lows to count

- Your income isn't consistent and yet you're doing everything those experts on Instagram have told you to

So what's missing?

I'll tell you....

It's YOU! You've lost sight of yourself. You've forgotten what really matters.

Your vision. Your dream. You.

Do it anyway!

You're going to inspire some people, and you're going to piss off the rest.

DO IT ANYWAY!

Never let what other people think hold you back.

Do what is right for YOU, and that is all you need to think about.

Treat yourself like a client

Sheesh. Why do you do this to yourself?

Logic and kindness with clients.

Shit and lies with yourself.

Bleurgh.

It's time to change that.

It's time to treat yourself like you would a client. Like you would a friend.

Can you do that?

No, I mean, like *actually* do it?

Let's make a pact right now to be kind and generous to ourselves.

Are you in?

DATA AND DREAMS

The data and numbers in your business might seem like the unsexy cousin you're forced to sit next to at a family wedding, but trust me, this is the unsung hero of your success and happiness.

Without knowing your numbers, and keeping an eye on them, you will miss opportunities to plug leaks, make gains, and genuinely build a business with your work/life balance in mind.

This section holds the true secret to you working less and earning more.

10k months? Pah!

You. Do. Not. Need. 10k. Months. As. Your. Goal.

Your goal is whatever you bloody well want it to be.

Working 3 days a week.

Having consistent energy.

Finding your mojo again.

Working from anywhere.

Pivoting your services.

Moving to the seaside.

Making more profit without more work.

Or, yes, 10k months, if that's genuinely what you want.

Goals are as personal as fingerprints.

A (slow!) runner's guide to goal setting

In September 2022, I completed my first parkrun since February 2020. To say I was out of practice at running was a bit of an understatement.

Guess what though? I ran that 5k parkrun without stopping.

Slooooowly, but still running. 42 minutes in fact, which is very slow for a 5k, but I still ran it all.

You see, that was the goal I set myself. I didn't want to walk, so slow-running got me to the 5k finish line, with an incredible sense of pride.

A friend of mine was doing 'couch to 5k' at the same time, and she ran for 30 minutes without stopping. I don't know how far she went as time was her goal.

Both of us smashed our goals (yay us!), but something about it is really interesting...

I wanted to finish the 5k without walking, and it took me 42 minutes. My friend wanted to run for 30 minutes without walking.

Without realising it, I had set a goal that was almost 50% higher than my friend's.

Interesting, eh?

See, it's the type of goal you set that could make all the difference to you. If I had said I wanted to run for 42 minutes without stopping, inner me would have immediately screamed "not on your nelly, mate!".

It's too long, it sounds too hard.

But to complete a 5k parkrun takes time out of the equation, and made it an easier thing for my brain to process. I didn't have to think. I didn't have to look at my watch. I just kept going until the finish line.

Slow and steady literally won the race.

An extra 50% might actually be achievable, if you just phrase it differently.

Turnover v profit

Turnover and profit are NOT the same thing...

TURNOVER is your sales —

ie money into your business. This is most likely what people are referring to when they talk about 10k months, but doesn't include what it costs to achieve those sales.

PROFIT is what's left —

after you've taken out costs for software, staff, ads, marketing, business lunches, stationery, equipment, etc etc etc. It's the money you can keep or reinvest into your business. It's really what matters!!

Without knowing how much it actually costs you to run your business, you might be working really hard in a business model that ain't never gonna make you any money.

You need to know your numbers.

It isn't boring or complicated either, I promise you. It's liberating, and pretty damn sexy to know you're on the right track, with no guesswork.

Whatever price you're thinking of, double it

Within a couple of months of starting my business, I had been asked enough times about social media management services to realise this could be a very lucrative string to my company's bow.

I had no clue how to price this though, so took advice from a friend who had a web design company, with a similar target audience. She said she knew lots of her clients would sign up for my social media management services if they were about £80 a month.

And lo, the price was set at £80 per month...

Now, anyone who has ever used social media in any shape or form will know that it takes time, commitment, and effort to create content, interact with followers, and reply to messages. Far more than £80 a month (for TWO platforms!) can get you, that's for sure.

But, when you're starting out, you don't really know what you're doing, and social media was still in its relative infancy then (2011), so this was all a big experiment.

Needless to say, I was inundated with clients. So much so that I had to take on my first member of staff to help me cope. We soon had about 40 companies on our books, and that was A LOT of work!

I eventually plucked up the courage to raise our prices to be more in line with the time and effort needed to service these clients.

By the time I stopped offering social media management as a service five years later, our top package was £2,500 a month, with the average package being about £600. Both a long way from £80!

Remember: time is a COST, and you have to charge for that.

If you're thinking of launching a new service, then I strongly suggest you double, or even triple, whatever price you're thinking of charging, because everything initially takes more effort than you think it will.

Get total clarity

What do you really want?

What sets your heart on fire?

What's your big vision?

Once you have total clarity on that, everything else falls into place.

I was talking to a brand new client the other day, and asked her what her really big goal was. She told me, and her face lit up as she was talking.

I then asked her how her current business model is getting her towards that dream.

And that's the moment it clicked. Her business wasn't in alignment with her big vision, which is why she was finding it hard to grow and scale.

Everything needs to be in alignment, and then it starts to feel easy.

Why you're not hitting your goals

Early on in my career, I sold advertising space for a big magazine publishing house in London. That meant targets and commission, and big fat financial goals.

I found the whole sales goal thing really dissatisfying though.

Not because I didn't ever hit them - I did and found it weirdly easy - but because it left me with a feeling of "yeah, and..?".

Once I had hit my monthly target, it all seemed a bit pointless. Sure, I could have earned more commission by carrying on selling, but I wasn't much motivated to do anything further once I had reached the point I needed to reach.

Quite simply, it was the wrong kind of goal for me.

If you're struggling to hit the goal you have set for yourself, then it could well be that it's just the wrong kind of goal to motivate you, and not that you're rubbish at what you do (I know you think this sometimes, and it simply isn't true).

Reframe your goal, and watch what a difference it makes.

You might just be surprised.

One step at a time

When my husband and I are out walking up some hill or fell or peak, we often come across rivers and streams that need to be crossed. I generally look for rocks in the water to make our route easier, but imagine if I didn't and each time I tried to cross in one big jump.

I would always give it a go, but likely end up rather soggy, and maybe with a broken ankle as well.

So why would you attempt to do the same thing in your business?

The other side of the river (AKA your goal) isn't reached in one big leap. It's achieved through about a million tiny steps.

Here's the guaranteed recipe for success:

✓ Decide on your goal
✓ Plan your route
✓ Start taking little actions

And then whadyaknow?

You'll be there before you know it.

Don't undervalue yourself

Undervaluing yourself and your skills and experience is all too common in business, especially amongst female business owners.

It makes it harder for you to attract clients, and it makes it harder for you to grow your business.

Pricing is always something I work on with my clients, and more often than not we end up doubling them (at the very least!).

That's not just to charge more for charging more's sake (ugh), but because your skills and experience should be reflected in your prices (yay).

You are incredibly special and talented, and deserve not to be undervalued – especially by yourself!!

Be intentional every day

If, like me, you are easily distracted by, well, anything... before you start doing something, ask yourself this simple question:

Is this activity going to help me reach my goal?

If the answer is yes, on you go!

If the answer is no, thank yourself for the brilliant idea or opportunity, and walk away.

It takes practice, but it is well worth it if you're serious about moving forward.

£6k in. £20k out.

It's 2016, and I have just made all my staff redundant.

Wait, this story gets cheerier!

This new, fresh, streamlined approach to business was different to what I had been building for the previous five years, and I wasn't quite sure what to do, or how to do it.

I got in touch with a coach I had been following on Facebook for a while. We talked, I liked her style, and I signed up to work with her for three months at £2k a month.

It was a BIG investment for me back then, but I knew I needed help to move forward, and I trusted this woman to deliver.

We had weekly Skype calls (soooo 2016!), at 7am for me as she was in Australia. Not ideal, but I soon realised it didn't matter if I turned up fresh out from under my duvet.

I didn't have to impress her; I was paying her to coach me. I could wear what the bloody hell I liked!

So, barriers down, we started work.

My coach helped me create an online programme, a structured live masterclass with an upsell into the programme (I am a trained tutor and had been running workshops for years, but this was subtly different), and a loose script for sales calls.

This sort of process wasn't anything like the norm it is now, so I knew I was ahead of the curve.

And I had a scalable product, that I could sell again and again.

Which I did!

Just in the three-month period I worked with my coach, I turned that £6k investment into £20k - not bad for 2016!

Without taking that massive financial leap of faith, I wouldn't have been such a forerunner in the online space, and I wouldn't have made as much money.

It's as simple as that.

I have told this story a lot over the years, as it is a real example of my empathy of knowing you need some guidance, but also to be shitting a brick about how much that support costs!

My experience is that the right coaching more than pays for itself in terms of cash, experience, and confidence.

Know your profit margin

When I hit my first decade in business in 2021, I looked back at my turnover, profit, and percentage profit from day one.

What's most striking about these numbers is that my professional annus horribilis (2015) was my highest turnover year, but the lowest profit. I actually made a loss of 3% that year, which is one of the reasons I made the decision to give up my expensive office and make my staff redundant.

BUT, if I just told you the big old six figure turnover number, you'd form a totally different opinion of how that year went. This is why you knowing ALL your numbers really does matter.

My overall profit margin over my first decade in business was 45.95%, but let's break that down even further:

In the year I become a solopreneur again (2016), the average was 58.7%.

And in the years since I started to feel truly happy in myself (2017 onwards), my average profit margin has increased to 77.55%.

Coincidence? I think not!

Being happy in your business doesn't just improve your health, it improves the profit margin too!

Vanity or sanity?

Would you rather have a 50k a year business where 80% of that is profit, or a 200k a year business where the profit is 20%?

They both give you 40k profit (cash) a year...

But one likely involves a lot more work than the other. And staff. And big outgoings...

So, the first option wins every time if you would like to work less and earn more.

Remember that profit matters far more than just having a big turnover.

Which option would you choose?

Are you optimising your 5-9am?

There is a TikTok trend called #my5to9 where people share how they optimise those early hours of 5am to 9am. You may have seen it or read about it.

Thing is, I hate the notion we have to optimise Every Single Minute of the day. Giving yourself and your mind the space to just breeeeeeeeathe, are some of the healthiest and most productive moments you'll have in any given day.

For me, 5am is absolutely a time for being asleep. 9am is a time for eating my breakfast. I don't put - nor do I want to put - anything else into that space.

And that doesn't mean anything at all. It doesn't mean I'm not successful; it doesn't mean I won't reach my goals; it doesn't mean that I'm not a dedicated coach to my clients.

What it does mean is that I don't start my day at 5am. Fact.

And the reason is simply because I don't want to. End of.

So, how do I optimise #my5to9? I don't, and you don't have to either.

Measure this, not that

Trying to grow your business using social media can be one of the most frustrating experiences you'll ever encounter.

You're doing All The Things, but NOTHING is happening...

What often happens is you create an account, start to post, get some likes and comments, get some new followers, see immediate progress, but then....

It gets hard.

You have to start repeating your message. Your follower count is crawling upwards. You're... BORED...

And this is when so many give up.

But what if you reflected in a more holistic way on how well you were doing?

What if you looked at the comments you had, and noted the specific words used, then created content including these, knowing it would resonate with your audience?

What if you looked at which posts got the most likes and repurposed them into new content, such as a video instead of a static image?

What if you looked at ALL the data – likes, comments, video views, shares, story replies, DMs, and, yes, your follower count – and realised that actually you've been doing an incredible job?

What if you realised you were closer to your goal than you thought, you'd just been looking at it the wrong way?

Celebrate each step of the way

I celebrate each and every new client who chooses to work with me.

Why?

It's one more business owner I am helping to reach their goals...

...and it's one more step towards me reaching mine.

Never say "it's one client but I really want 20" or "I am still so far from what I want to achieve"

Take time to celebrate each step of your journey.

You do that for your clients, so give yourself the same treatment.

You don't have to "smash it" to be successful

Social media is full of people giving you advice on how to SMASH IT, but what if that expression doesn't resonate with you?

What if you prefer working in a gentler, quieter way?

Does that mean you can't be successful?

ABSOLUTELY NOT!

Success means a very different thing to us all, and it certainly doesn't have to be measured by the number of hours you work, or how hard you hustle.

That can just create noise. And noise can be stressful.

I'm an introvert, so I have learnt how to manage my energy so that when I have been "on" for a while, I know I need to plan in time to be "off" and recharge.

Is that "smashing it"?

No, it's not.

But it IS quietly moving forward towards a clearly defined goal, in a way that I can control and - yes -

allows me to be successful according to my personal definition of what that means to me and my family.

If you're someone who thrives on smashing it, or hustling, or bossing it, then I salute you and your energy and confidence.

If you're someone who prefers quiet, gentle, smart and sustainable progress, then you're in the right place.

Less is more

In the summer of 2021, my husband and I went to a festival. It was the first chance to see live music and comedy since the pandemic started.

The main BIIIIIG difference to a pre- or post-pandemic festival was the allocation of individual camping pitches that you could park your car on too.

And....

YOUR OWN TOILET!!!

Oh yes, that deserves to be in capital letters, as anyone who has been to a festival knows.

It was actually more expensive to attend than in 2019, despite there being fewer acts and less to do. But, YOUR OWN TOILET made it worth ten times the price!

All this got me thinking.

Are you trying to offer too much to your customers?

Would they actually pay more for less, if it's exactly the thing they want and need? Do they want their own toilet and are they prepared to pay for it?

My guess is yes. I know my clients do. They want

access to me, my ideas, my solutions, my caring support, my belief in them, the transformation they get. That's about as straightforward as you can get, and it's what they want. And yes, they are prepared to pay for that.

So, how can you change what you offer to make it more of a VIP experience? Imagine having fewer customers but a higher income. That is your work less, earn more dream coming true...

Can I just manifest it?

Without an ultimate goal or vision for your life and business, you really are just wishing on a star.

How will you know if what you're doing each day will get you there, if you don't know what "there" looks like?

You need a goal FIRST, and THEN you can focus on manifesting it (making it happen).

Feel the fear and do it anyway

I promise you, there is absolutely no reason why you can't achieve what you want to achieve, but the fear in your heart may tell you otherwise.

Our excuses for not doing things are often what surfaces out of fear. Fear of failure, and fear of success. Big fat fear.

My clients have presented a multitude of fear-based reasons for not doing things over the years, including:

- I don't have 10,000 followers so I can't do that
- I don't understand the technology so I can't do that
- People who wear glasses can't do that
- Everyone will laugh at me if I do that
- I don't charge enough to do that
- I'm not experienced enough to do that
- I have too much experience and will be seen as a dinosaur if I do that
- Everyone is much cooler than me so I can't do that
- I can't do that because I am a woman

Can you see that pattern? All of these things are perceived issues and not actual real facts. They are all stories we tell ourselves to protect us from what MIGHT happen.

But what if you sat with these feelings for a while and then took a deep breath, mustered all your courage, and just did whatever it is that you want to do?

I tell you how that would feel.... truly terrifying... but *an INCREDIBLE step towards the life you are dreaming of.*

Just keep going

Let me take you back to June 1986.

It was a warm summer's day, and I was in the fourth year of primary school. It was cross country day. I went to a tiny village primary school, so there were probably only 20 or so kids running the course, but I remember it as being a big and exciting event, with hundreds of supporters lining the route...

The race started at the local park and went across the fields, past the school, then around the village and back to the playing fields. We didn't really know how far the route was, or even what we were doing, but we were ready!

And off we went! Running as fast as our little 11-year-old legs could carry us.

But then, something odd happened. There was a hill partway round and most of my fellow pupils stopped to walk.

I remember as clearly as if it were yesterday saying to my friends "why are you stopping?"

"We're tired. This is hard" they replied.

I was confused as I really wanted to see that finish line, so I just carried on running. Off I went on my own. Past the school, round the corner, down the lane, back onto the village playing fields.

I just didn't stop. I kept going. I had my goal in sight.

And I WON! Yes, little 11-year-old me came first in the school cross country.

I didn't know the route.

I didn't know the distance.

But I was focused on finishing, so I just kept going.

And won.

This is exactly what it's like to run a business. You don't always know the route or the distance. There will be hills to climb and lots of people will give up at that point.

But if you're clear on what you want to achieve, then you can get over any obstacle or challenge. If you *don't* know what you want, you're likely to give up because it's *too hard* and you can't see the end goal.

Celebrate what you've achieved

It's generally only when we take time to look back at our business and life journey that we think "wow, how the heck did I achieve that?", but we should be celebrating what we achieve on a daily basis.

Let's normalise "I did an amazing job today"...

The secret to 315% month-on-month growth

In 2022, after a conscious pivot from being a marketing coach, to a business coach and mentor, I knew things were going well.

Saying things are "going well" means nothing though, and so I decided to put some figures to that. I wanted to know exactly how well things were going.

I took my sales totals for April, May, June, and July-to-the-date-of-the-exercise, worked out the percentage increase month-on-month, and calculated the average of that.

315% average monthly growth. WTAF??!!!

Yeah, so things were going pretty damned well, I'd say. (For transparency - my profit margin generally sits around the 75% mark)

And do you know what the secret is behind this success?

Doing what makes me happy. Yep, that's it. Pure and simple. I hadn't been in love with marketing for a looooooong time, so I gave myself permission to help my clients with all aspects of business, and I am absolutely bloody loving it.

My clients are getting results, and so am I.

Everyone wins, and that's the way it should be in business.

I did this exercise because someone asked me how it was going. Sometimes it takes someone else saying something, or asking you a particular question, to make you realise how far you have come.

What goal has this chapter helped you set?

Do you know what your profit margin is, and what you would like it to be?

How do you feel right now?

EASY MARKETING

The simple fact of the matter is, in order to sell more of your services or products, you need to tell more people about them.

Business success is nothing more fancy than that, when you boil it down to its bare bones (despite what you might see or hear on social media!).

The very mention of the word 'marketing' might have you running for the hills, but in the final part of this book, you will see that there is a much easier way to approach it all.

After reading this section, you will actually dare to put yourself out there, and be able to be market consistently without feeling exhausted or paralysing yourself with self-criticism.

Ready?

It's all marketing

Without marketing, none of us would have businesses. That is a fact!

You might not always think of your marketing as marketing, but I promise you it is...

There are the obvious kinds:

- social media
- websites
- podcasts

And then there are the kinds that can be so crucial for building businesses, but often get overlooked:

- talking to people
- joining in
- having fun
- living life

All these are forms of marketing. They are all infectious parts of you, and your love of life and your business.

No, they aren't covered in traditional marketing courses, but they are often more important than making sure your website is the whizziest possible, or that your social media feed looks the prettiest it can.

This kind of marketing is heart-centred. It's

passionate. It makes people want to know more...

And THAT is what marketing is all about.

Go out there and enjoy your business and your life, without feeling guilty, and just watch what happens.

This will change your life

I am sick to death of all the slimy nonsense that's thrown about on social media.

"Have guaranteed 10k months using my fool-proof system!"

"How to work from the beach for two hours a day and make 1million"

"Get 100k followers following my 30-day plan"

It's all BULLSHIT!!

You can't just snap your fingers and make 6-figures overnight. I would love to be able to tell you the secret of that, but I can't, because I really don't think it exists.

I can tell you what does work though....

✓ Knowing who you're talking to.
✓ Creating useful and interesting content.
✓ Making offers over and over again.

This is how I get new clients. This is how I make money.

There's no insane 24/7 hustle. There are no

horrendously unachievable deadlines.

Just a nice gentle growth, a steady stream of customers, and a quiet confidence that it is all going according to plan.

Get clear on what you do

If you're struggling to get clients, chances are you're not really clear about what it is you actually do.

Not being clear in your own head means you haven't got a hope in hell of being clear to anyone in your marketing. And woolly marketing is time consuming, stressful, and utterly pointless.

I'm not saying you need to totally nail a niche, but you do need to know what kind of people you help, with what, and with what result. Without that, you are always going to struggle to get clients, because no one will know you're talking to them, and won't be able to self-identify as someone who needs you.

In a coaching call with a client recently, she said she had gone into a panic when someone had asked her what she did. *What did she do? How did she help people? Aaaaaaaargh!*

So we worked on her "I help..." statement. In under 10 minutes, we had nailed down exactly who she helped, to achieve what, which means that...

The relief on her face was palpable. She can now speak with confidence to the people she wants to work with, knowing what specific thing she helps them with, and what it will empower them to do better in the future.

Once you have your "I help..." statement clear in your mind, your marketing becomes easy-peasy.

No more time wasting, no more woolliness, and loads more enquiries!

How to deal with a crowded niche

If you're worried that your niche is crowded, you're right, it probably is.

Whaaaaaaat???? You won't hear many coaches saying that, I know!

Honestly though, it doesn't matter.

There is only one you, and that's why clients choose to work with you.

Just be you and don't worry about anyone else.

How to make social media easy

✓ Make sure your content is relevant

Think about the topic your audience is expecting you to talk about, and don't deviate too far from that.

✓ Start conversations, don't preach

Remember you're on social media to be social, so think about starting conversations, not just sharing everything you know.

✓ Post with purpose

Your overall objective is to grow your business, so think about what your post will achieve.

It's a sensible sales strategy to signpost people to a useful piece of content, or a free download or masterclass, or to chat in the DMs.

No need to edit

When you create content from your heart, content that is truly aligned with your values and identity, why would you want to chop it about and edit it?

Part of being truly YOU, is being honest about who you are.

I don't believe that any of us need to edit ourselves.

I believe we are all amazing just as we are.

If you want to edit, go ahead. That is cool. It's your choice.

BUT if you DON'T want to edit, you do not need to. That's one simple way you can take pressure off yourself and make business just a little bit easier.

Don't post more, post better

It may be tempting to post more and more often if you're not generating clients from your social media content

BUT

If you're not getting clients - or starting interesting conversations with the right audience - with the content you're currently sharing...

...sharing more of it won't make a jot of difference.

You'll just get
- burnt out
- exhausted
- pissed off
- scared
- confused
- and want to give up

The problem isn't with how often you're sharing content.

The problem is with WHAT you're sharing.

Look at who you're talking to and what they want to hear from you, and share that!

Small audience? Who cares!

Do you sometimes feel like you're cursed with a small audience?

It's easy to fall into that trap, because social media is full of people promising they'll get you to 10k followers...

What if I told you that you don't need that many people to be a success?

You already have a BEAUTIFUL audience, even if it's only 400 people.

That's a lot of people if they were all lined up outside your house...

Chasing new people won't get you ahead.

Nurturing and caring for the audience you already have, will.

How are you feeling
right now?

Take a moment to
notice and write down
the positives, the
negatives, and what
support you need.

Some simple content ideas

One of the most frequent questions I get asked is "what do I post on social media?" so here are a few ideas:

1. Introduce yourself

Your new followers might not know much about you, so say hello, and remind existing followers who the heck you are and what you do. Share something about you to start a conversation.

2. Interview someone

Got a client or follower who's doing good things? Do a live interview with them and share the inside story. Lives are a great way to talk to yours and your interviewee's audience.

3. Go behind the scenes

What really happens in your business? That's what we all want to know! Share the info in a timelapse video, talking to camera, or a series of images in a carousel post.

4. Share a 'before and after'

What results do your clients get after working with you? Or how do you turn a jumble of thoughts/paper/ wool into something structured/tidy/creative? Show us. The creative journey is always interesting.

5. **Create an 'ask me anything' post**

Give your followers an open space to chat with you. They will learn, and you will get some great content for future posts. Win win.

6. **Share top tips**

You're the expert. Share useful tips that will help people move forward. They will thank you! Make a list of all your FAQs and break them down into little tips to make your content easier to digest.

7. **Create a 'how to' video**

Some people learn better from video so create a little demo. Getting a visual of your work really helps cement what you do in people's minds.

8. **Share a testimonial**

Clients saying good things about you? Shout it from the rooftops! Screenshot DMs or emails and add them to a Canva graphic in your branding colours.

9. **Tell people what you sell...**

Don't forget to remind people how they can buy from you or sign up to work with you.

When you get nothing but tumbleweed

Sharing a post on social media and getting nothing back but crickets or tumbleweed happens to everyone, don't worry! Sometimes some content resonates more than others, and sometimes people simply just don't see what you post.

Don't worry about it.

As long as you are generally getting some engagement, and that engagement leads to interesting conversations (and eventually some clients), then you're on the right track.

Being passionate about what you do, and showing that in your content, will beat any algorithm in the long run.

Just stick with it, and look at the overall picture, not just a one-hit wonder (or flop!).

Take a break. Please!

I'm going to say it straight... If you need to have a rest, please have a rest!

And if that rest includes a couple of days of not posting on social media, THAT IS FINE!

Your followers will still be there for you if you don't post every single day.

I promise you it really is ok to take a few days away. Living life is important. Working on your business is important.

Take the time when you need the time.

Look after yourself and your business will look after you...

I deleted my Facebook group

I have deleted my free Facebook group. It's gone. Forever.

There is a lot of talk about the need to have a group in order to grow a coaching (or indeed any!) business, so why have I gone against this advice?

Well... In all honesty, I didn't know what to do with the group.

There were certainly some truly lovely people in there. Some had been clients a decade ago. Some had been clients in the last year or so. Some had signed up for my freebies. Some had connected with me randomly on Instagram.

But I didn't know how to pull them all together.

Well, I mean, I did know, of course. Post lots of engaging content, share lots of useful info, start conversations... Knowing what to do isn't all that hard, it's the DOING it that counts.

And I didn't.

I love talking to people by email. I love sharing things on Instagram and making friends there. Heck, I am even falling back in love with LinkedIn. But my free Facebook group?

Nah.

I just couldn't even seem to make it part of my daily business life.

It was a thing I thought "oh shit, I haven't shared anything in there for ages" about. And that is NOT good. It was a disservice to those lovely folks inside the group, and it was a pointless stresser on my plate.

Since 2009, I have been telling clients to pick one social media platform and do it well, and I know I do Insta well. I do emails well. I am starting to get back to doing LinkedIn well. I have a great weekly podcast (like this book, it's called Life In Business. Find it and have a listen).

And that's enough.

It is ok to step back from things that are no longer serving you or your business. Even if you're being told by "the experts" that you need to do them.

You don't.

Pick one (or two) and do it well, and your to-do list will be shorter... Oh, and it'll make your business grow faster too.

Doing less is magic!

So, goodbye Facebook group. Hello a bit more headspace. I call that a win.

Be like a cup of coffee

I've noticed over the years, that at in-person events people will often head straight for the coffee machine. They like that caffeine hit: it makes them feel better.

Imagine your content is that cup of coffee.

When people see your content, they immediately feel better. They immediately feel like they've had their hit. They immediately feel as if they've been understood, they've been seen. Somebody gets them. It's what they need.

If you're thinking content-first, not feeling-first, this won't happen, because what you're sharing is too process-driven.

By stopping thinking about content as something that you have to create because it's on your to-do list, you're actually then focusing on your audience, and what it is that they want to see or hear, and what it is that they want to feel.

What you're focusing on then is how can you communicate this feeling of, "yes, I feel understood!"

Sometimes the way to resonate with people is to encourage them NOT to do things rather than telling them what to do.

So if you're telling people what to do all the time with how-to lessons and tutorials, it's more stuff that they've got to do. It's just more stuff, more stuff, more stuff, more stuff.

If you stop telling people more things they need to do in order to be better, people will respond to you more warmly, because you're making them feel better. You're taking something off their plate, exactly like I'm doing to you here today.

I'm reframing for you how to think about your content differently so that you're not just thinking about it as creating content, you're thinking of it as a way to easily connect with your audience.

It stops being a chore. And you feel understood.

Be honest. Always

I love the countryside. I love views. I love space. I love fresh air. So, when my husband said he needed to be in Wales all week for work, I jumped at the chance to go with him to get my fix of scenery.

I spent a bit of time on Airbnb, looking for properties within a 10-mile radius of where he needed to be, and one jumped right out at me. The description and pictures made it look perfect: it was totally self-contained and private; had an outside seating area; superfast broadband (essential so I could work!); and views to die for.

I booked it there and then for five nights.

When we arrived, we got a bit of a shock. The place itself only had a small window in the bedroom and a patio door from the lounge, both of which looked out onto a wall. The kitchen and bathroom didn't have any windows at all.

There was a view, but you had to go outside to the car park to see it. Er, what?! That is NOT what the listing led me to believe.

So, I spent almost a week in a dingy converted garage, with nothing but a rendered wall and some railings to inspire me. At least the broadband was reasonably reliable though!

The moral of this sorry tale is that you must
ALWAYS *be honest in your marketing.*

Don't over-promise and under-deliver or, quite frankly,
people will be pissed off with you, write bad reviews,
tell everyone about their experience, and generally
think you're a bit of a con artist.

Social media doesn't have to be hard work

With over a decade of experience researching, watching, learning and teaching, I can tell you with some authority that social media can be really hard work.

Is the solution to walk away from Instagram and Facebook because we don't have any energy left from everything else life throws at us?

It could be, but there is always a way to approach social media that makes it considerably less hard work...

You could take a step back, forget all the lip-syncing and dancing, and actually think about what you're trying to achieve.

Let's put it into a real-life scenario: If you met someone at an event/party/supermarket and they seemed like someone you'd love to work with, what would you do? I'd hazard a guess that you'd start a nice conversation with them, ask a few questions, and get to know them a bit.

You would be human, and have a wonderful human interaction that would enrich both your lives a little bit.

So why do we make social media any different?

Why do we MAKE it hard work?

Why don't we treat it as hundreds of mini-encounters with our fellow humans?

Imagine the magic that would create!

Now that's not hard work.

That's enlightening.

That's enriching.

That's empowering.

And that's how to grow a business too.

1% of followers gone in a day

I lost 1% of my Instagram followers in one day!

1% doesn't sound like a massive percentage, but it's quite a lot all at once. But you know what? I'm actually happy about it.

What happened, pure and simple, is that I put an offer out there. No sugar coating. Just a post saying here I am, and here's how you can work with me to get you moving towards that big beautiful goal of yours.

And some of my followers didn't like it. 1% in fact. They unfollowed me.

(For comparison, I emailed the exact same offer to my lovely email subscribers, and I had just 0.03% - a perfectly normal and average amount - who unsubscribed from future emails)

So why on earth does losing 1% make me happy?

Well, if I put an offer out there after sharing interesting, funny, engaging, and useful content on a daily basis for years, and it causes someone to hit the unfollow button, we are clearly not in perfect alignment, and I'm not the coach for them.

And that's cool.

They've got the value and insight they wanted from all my free content, and it's time for them to move on.

No hard feelings.

It makes more room for someone new who I can get to know and support, and maybe work with one day.

Don't ever be afraid to put an offer out there, because you are running a business, not volunteering. It's not your job to provide endless free stuff.

You deserve to be paid – and paid well – for what you do.

So keep on sharing your magic and don't sweat the 1% who choose to say goodbye.

There are lots more of the perfect person for you out there, just you wait and see.

How to conquer your fear of going live

Do you have a fear of going live on social media or recording videos to upload to Instagram, LinkedIn or Facebook?

Let me give you a little insider secret that will tell you how to conquer your fear of going live.

It's simple...

Imagine you are FaceTiming a friend or client, and just talking to that one person.

And that's it!

Yes, the secret to conquering your fear is that simple, but *the best insider tricks and tips often are the simplest things*, it's just that we can't always see them because we're so focused on the fear, and not the solution.

Going live or sharing talk-to-camera videos is a brilliant way to not only share your message, but it allows people to get to know you a little bit better, and see how you speak and act, which can absolutely influence whether they want to work with you or not.

It also is one of the key factors in building trust.

So forget about the fact you might be broadcasting live to 3 or 10 or 100 people, and instead think about the exact same content as a one-to-one FaceTime conversation with a well-liked client or friend.

I promise you this trick will make it easier for you.

The downside to lip syncing

Lip syncing is BIG business on Instagram, but if that is all you do, you might actually be creating a barrier between you and your audience.

Think about it...

No one explains things in quite the same way as you, or has quite the same experience as you, or helps people in quite the same way as you.

So why would you want to dilute that incredible magic with lip syncs All. The. Time?

If you're always lip syncing and never speaking with your own voice, people might not know what your tone or emotion is like, or what your true voice is.

That stuff matters!

It helps us connect and get to know each other. It helps us build trust.

It helps us say yes to wanting to work with each other.

So lip sync away, but don't forget to add a big healthy dose of YOU to the mix as well.

Don't trick people onto your email list

Unsubscribing from an email list can be a really positive thing to do. I am on loads of people's email lists as they can be a very useful source of ideas and inspiration, and every so often I go through them all and take myself off the lists that are no longer relevant, useful or interesting.

In doing this I have discovered some downright unethical tactics.

One such example, from a leading American expert in the world of online marketing, is so terrible, I need to share it with you:

I clicked the unsubscribe button at the bottom of this guy's email and it opened a web page which asked me to enter my name and email address, rather than picking it up automatically. I was a bit irritated by this but duly entered it and clicked the unsubscribe button.

This then opened a web page, which was a bit weird because it is normal to see a confirmation of unsubscribing page.

About 10 minutes later, I got an email from this guy, thanking me for requesting his latest PDF guide.

Whaaaaat? No, I unsubscribed!

I then had another email from him, with the subject line "I'm a failure". I expected this to be an apology for the automated unsubscribe error, but no, it was a sales email. Hmmm. So, I scrolled to the bottom and once again clicked the unsubscribe button. The page opened and I started to type in my email address again, but this time I noticed his downright sneaky tactic...

The button you clicked after putting in your email address didn't say unsubscribe, it said subscribe.

That's a dirty trick.

I think he (rightly!) assumed that no one reads the text on an unsubscribe page and so tweaked his content so he actually got you to opt in to a new list. That isn't good practice. Sure, it will build up the number of people on your email list, but people who don't want to receive your content.

I, for one, would not want to take advice from this "expert" if that is their standard business growth tactic. It's deceitful and disrespectful to his audience.

Honesty in your marketing is always the way to win friends and influence people. Choose that approach instead!

Your follower count doesn't matter

So often people say to me "I don't have many followers on social media", with a forlorn look on their face.

I'm here to tell you that it doesn't matter half as much as you think!

What matters is the friendships you create. The comments you get. The DMs. That's what's really important.

Look at it this way: which of these scenarios is more likely to turn a follower into a client?

a) 5,500 followers; average 50 likes per post; or

b) 300 followers; average 50 likes per post AND 10 comments AND two DMs?

Now can you see which numbers really matter?

Your audience are people not numbers

How does the number of likes, comments and saves you get on your posts actually translate into people's online behaviour? Let me break it down for you.

Likes

A 'like' is someone just scrolling and nodding and smiling. If you think of it in real world terms, imagine walking along the street and seeing someone you know, nodding 'alright?' at them and walking on.

Comments

Comments are conversation starters, as well as confirmation that your content is resonating with your audience.

You can reply to comments and really start to get to know people. Note: people, not numbers!

Saves

People who save your posts are the ones who are filing it away for future use. They think it's so valuable, or inspiring, or useful that they want to be able to access it over and over again.

Saves are fantastic! These people value you.

Messages and DMs

Ooh, the delicious sign that someone really, REALLY, likes what you're saying and wants to chat directly with you. Once someone has popped into your DMs, you can continue to talk to them, or share links with them, and useful content, or send voice notes, and really become their go-to person.

And that's when the sales start to explode!

Remember that every single piece of engagement is from a person who has felt seen by what you're sharing. You don't need 15,000 people. You need ones and twos whose lives you can really improve.

The magic is in the small numbers.

Look at the numbers as people. Nurture them. Be thankful for each and every one.

A simple way to get more customers

A simple way to get more customers is to make it easier for people to buy.

Don't bury your sign up, register, or buy buttons. Make them BIG and obvious!

The easier you make it for people to buy from you or sign up with you, the more clients you will get.

She left her husband

A few years ago, a client came to me because she wanted to create a marketing strategy for her business.

We talked a lot about her business, but I didn't feel it was a mind-blowingly transformational session. I felt there was something deeper to uncover. Marketing strategy wasn't actually what was going to make a difference to her.

And then she said it:

"I find it hard to work from home outside of traditional working hours"

Cue the coaching questions from me...

What did she want her working day to look like?

What hours would suit her?

Did her work make her happy?

What was it about working from home that didn't work for her?

Our session became emotional and she poured her heart out about no longer feeling in sync with her husband, and what her dream life actually looked like.

It wasn't the one she was living, and that was holding her business back...

Through our conversation, my client gave herself permission to admit she wanted to leave her husband. She had come to me with what she thought was the problem - a lack of marketing strategy - and I had helped her realise that a marketing strategy was just a sticking plaster.

What she needed to do was be happy in herself.

And <u>that</u> was what would allow her, and her business, to thrive!

Not every session ends with something so radical (!!), but I do always get below the surface with my clients to help them uncover what it is they really want to change.

It's powerful. It's magic. And I love it!

What really happens when you go viral

I recently went viral on Instagram. Properly small-business-viral. I'm talking almost-1000-times-my-total-followers viral.

It's the dream, right? And it happened to me. After over a decade of sharing content online, finally it was my time.

I had made it. This was the catalyst to ev-er-y-thing. The world really was my oyster now.

Or was it....?

Well, no, *of course* it wasn't. It doesn't mean anything in the grand scheme of things.

Sure, I got a decent number of I'm-scrolling-by-but-I'll-give-this-a-like likes on the Reel, but only three comments. That's a shocking engagement rate so clearly shows the right people weren't being shown it. Gotta love an algorithm.

But what about all the new followers I gained from thousands and thousands of new-to-me Instagram people seeing my content?

I got two new followers.

TWO.

But the momentum from that viral Reel will have given my subsequent content a nice big boost, no?

No.

My next Reel, shared the very next day, jumped straight over that viral wave, and crashed down at a reach of 293 people. 293!

Going viral is nothing other than a fun few hours watching the numbers go up and up. It doesn't mean anything for you and your business in the long run.

Connections and conversations are what matter, and are what will make a difference. They are what will spark an idea, or determine a path, or grow a business.

Start conversations with your new followers and don't worry about the thousands of randoms who may or may not see what you're sharing.

It's not the how, it's the what

HOW you show up online doesn't really matter.

WHAT you say really does.

People need to CARE about what you're saying.

They need to KNOW you're talking to THEM.

You need to make people feel EMOTION.

HOW you do this though, is up to you.

Videos, Reels, blogs, photos, quotes, graphics… You get to choose what you like doing.

It's not the HOW that will get you new clients…

It's the WHAT.

Could a "so what?" save your business?

When you're in the middle of a panic about so-and-so having more likes on Instagram than you, or you really (and I mean *really*) hate going live, I want you to pause for a moment and say to yourself...

...so what?

So what if so-and-so has more likes? You have absolutely no idea if any of those likes convert to customers. (S)he might make zero money and all those likes are just vanity metrics.

So what if you hate going live? It is a brilliant way to grow your audience, but if you really hate it *(rather than being terrified of it; the two are very different)* then there are lots of other ways you can market yourself and your business.

So what? is an incredibly powerful question to ask yourself.

It's the difference between paralysis from comparisonitis, and actual proper positive steps forward in a way that suits you.

It's your business, and so what if you're doing things differently?

Welcome to working less, earning more, and embracing true happiness!

Resources

Hover your phone's camera over these QR codes to get access to some incredible FREE resources.

37 Simple-To-Implement Ways To Make Your Business Easier This Week

I know you want an easy business and an easy life.

I know you completely understand the concept of making things easier.

And I also know you struggle with actually implementing things in an easy way!

You have all the good intentions, but somehow everything just gets bigger and bigger, and more complex, and before you know it you have just created yet another layer of overwhelm.

That stops today.

This guide contains 37 really straightforward ways to make your business easier this week.

These things are so simple to implement, that all you have to do is read the list and you'll find you've made mindset changes before you have even got to the end!

7 Easy Steps To Starting An Email List That Gets You Clients!

You want an easier way to grow your business than having to spend hours on social media, dancing and lip syncing, or being preyed on by hackers or spambots, yes?

Well, email is your answer!

Emails are seen - unlike about 90% of social media posts.

Emails are digested at a reader's own pace - unlike social media posts which scroll by in a blur, never to be found again.

Emails can be intimate and personal - unlike social media posts which are shared to many.

Emails are simple - no videos to record.

This guide walks you through the simplest way to start an email list that gets you clients, and the best thing is you can be up and running by the end of today!

About the Author

Libby Langley is an award-winning business coach, podcaster, and author of Life In Business - the first of many sanity-saving books for female entrepreneurs.

Since starting her business in 2011, Libby has experienced every twist and turn of the self-employed roller coaster, making her a true expert in the field of been-there-done-that. Her honesty, vulnerability, and humour give credence to her incredible ability to offer practical solutions to almost any business scenario.

With a focus on working less and earning more, Libby wears her Queen of Easy Business crown with pride as she helps women transform their businesses from over-complicated and hard work, to profitable and deeply enjoyable.

Libby lives on the edge of the Peak District with her husband and cat.

Find her at www.libbylangley.com

libbylangley

Life In Business podcast

Acknowledgements

Turns out there is a hell of a lot more work behind the scenes to creating a book than just typing a few thousand sentences into Word! And so, Clare McCabe – thank you for being a brilliant book coach. Your support and 'just bloody sit down and write' voice notes have been invaluable.

Malini, and Steven, all I can say is it's amazing what can be achieved through FB Messenger! Thank you for not being too afraid to challenge me when you could see something I couldn't.

Helen Rowan and I met on LinkedIn, and as soon as I knew this book was going to be an actual real thing, I raced to her photographic studio to get 'the cover shot'. Thank you, Helen, you are an incredible talent.

Thanks to Mum and Dad for supporting me through all my years in business, despite not really having a clue what I do. Now you can proudly say you have a daughter who's a published author, and everyone will know what you mean.

And finally, thank you to Jon, the love of my life. You make me laugh every day, even when times are a bit shitty. You have believed in me since the day we started our lives together, and I am forever grateful we are by each other's sides, making the best team in the world. I love you, boo.

Printed in Great Britain
by Amazon